THE MINISTRY OF GOD'S PEOPLE

Donna M. Costa

DISCIPLESHIP RESOURCES
MATERIALS FOR GROWTH IN CHRISTIAN FAITH AND LIFE
P.O. Box 189 • Nashville, TN 37202 • Phone (615) 340-7284

On the cover: Ministry occurs in all settings of life. This image of the various settings for Christian life and service is adapted from the graphic logo used by the Section on Ministry of the Laity, General Board of Discipleship.

Unless otherwise noted, all scripture quotations are from the New Revised Standard Version of the Holy Bible, copyright © 1989 by the Division of Christian Education of the National Council of the Churches of Christ in the United States of America.

Library of Congress Catalog Card No. 91-75146

ISBN 0-88177-108-2

DR108B

CONTENTS

FOREWORD   *v*

INTRODUCTION   *vii*

SESSION 1
Images of Our Calling   1

SESSION 2
Called and Gifted   9

SESSION 3
Called to Be Servants   20

SESSION 4
Called to Grow in Grace   29

SESSION 5
Called to Covenant   37

LEADER'S NOTES   47

ENDNOTES   49

FOR FURTHER READING   51

FOREWORD

I t is common in The United Methodist Church to hear affirmations of the "ministry of all Christians." But this phrase is imaged differently by different people. What images help us in new understandings of ministry? And how can we act more effectively out of our belief that all of God's people are called to love and to serve? This study provides an opportunity for persons to explore images of ministry and to accept their call to minister.

The study process has been prepared by Donna Costa, a former conference lay leader and student of ministry of the laity, in collaboration with three units in the General Board of Discipleship—the Section on Ministry of the Laity, the Section on Christian Education and Age-Level Ministries, and Discipleship Resources. It is a direct response to General Conference action in 1988. That Conference approved and referred to the General Board of Discipleship a request for a churchwide congregationally based study on the general ministry of all Christian believers.

Special thanks to Evelyn Burry, Alyne JoAnn Eslinger, John Gooch, Craig Gallaway, David Hazlewood, and Roy Ryan who helped shape both content and process, and to all of the staff in Discipleship Resources who made certain that the text was readable and accurate.

I commend this book for your individual and small group study.

All God's People in
All Places,
And in
All Times,
Are Called to Love
And to Serve.

DAVID L. WHITE
Assistant General Secretary
Section on Ministry of the Laity
General Board of Discipleship

INTRODUCTION

On Laity Sunday in 1976, I preached a sermon as the lay leader of my congregation. The text suggested in *the Interpreter* magazine was 1 Peter 2:9-10:

> But you are a chosen race, a royal priesthood, a holy nation, God's own people, in order that you may proclaim the mighty acts of him who called you out of darkness into his marvelous light. Once you were not a people, but now you are God's people; once you had not received mercy, but now you have received mercy.

Following the service, a retired clergy person, who served as our minister of visitation, told me I had done a good job and asked, "Have you ever considered going into the ministry?"

Somewhat taken aback, I answered that I had enough to do with my life already—raising a family, serving my congregation, working with a local environmental group, and maintaining relationships with friends, neighbors, and extended family.

On later reflection, though, I realized I was angry and disappointed. The very point of the scripture and the sermon, it seemed to me, was that all those accepted into God's family as sons and daughters, and heirs of Christ, were called to be God's own people, a holy nation, a royal priesthood. That meant that as a Christian, I already *was* in ministry—dedicating and using my gifts and my life for the glory of God in many arenas and with many people, proclaiming the "mighty acts" of God.

The next week, I sought out this pastor who had challenged me. "I've thought about your question," I told him, "and I've decided that I already *am* in ministry."

All of God's people are ministers. This was an essential principle in the New Testament church. It is also the guiding vision of this study. The vision itself is clear from scripture:

> But *each of us* was given grace according to the measure of Christ's gift. . . . The gifts he gave were that some would be apostles, some prophets, some evangelists, some pastors and teachers, to equip the saints *for the work of the ministry,* for building up the body of Christ, until all of us come to the unity of the faith and of the knowledge of the Son of God, to maturity, to the measure of the full stature of Christ (Ephesians 4:7, 11-13).

Each of us is given grace for the work of the ministry: That's the vision. Each of us has a part to play in God's purpose for the church and for the world in Christ. As clear as the vision is in scripture, however, it is not always so clear in practice. All too often we have accepted a much more limited vision of gifts and ministry.

This study is one of personal discovery, to be carried out alone as well as with a small group. We will use biblical study, personal reflection, group discussion, art, and liturgy to enable all participants to "do" theology—to develop their own understandings of what it means to be in ministry as the people of God.

Who is the church? What are your spiritual gifts? How do the gifts of lay people connect with those of the clergy? What is ministry—"in the world" as well as "in the church"? These are the questions that summon our discovery. Your own experiences, dreams, creativity, and openness will shape your responses to the call of the Spirit.

The study is divided into five sessions. In each session there are four steps: (1) a focus statement, (2) a guide for group discussion, (3) a design for worship (hymn numbers refer to *The United Methodist Hymnal*), and (4) an assignment in preparation for the next session. The focus statement introduces basic issues. Discussion questions lead into group experiences of worship, celebration, and covenant. A special dimension of this study is the opportunity to work with a group of people and to grow together as you share and deepen your own covenants to be in ministry.

This study can be used in a variety of ways. As a congregational or neighborhood group study, you might plan to meet once each week for five weeks, at a time convenient to all. You should plan for one and a half to two hours for each session. If your group consists of more than seven people, divide again into groups of four. This will leave time for everyone to enter into the discussion. Depending on the level of interest in your congregation, you could have several groups going at the same time.

Another possibility would be to use the study in a retreat setting. This would be an excellent resource for a spiritual life retreat for any of a number of groups in the congregation, such as a Sunday school class or the leadership council of the congregation. The material of the study would have to be tailored to fit the schedule of your retreat, but in any case you should allot at least two full days in order to use the study effectively.

As for leadership, your pastor may need to be involved in some sessions (for example, Session 5). But because the focus is on the ministry of all of God's people, don't miss the opportunity to involve lay leadership as well. General leader's instructions for all sessions are provided on pp. 47-48. More specialized instructions are included at appropriate places throughout the study.

In preparation for this study, I recommend that you plan an organizational meeting. The objectives of this meeting should be: (1) to introduce the workbook, (2) to test the interest of prospective participants, (3) to determine who will covenant to complete the study together, (4) to take orders for workbooks if these have not already been purchased, and (5) to set an appropriate time and place for meetings. (Be sure to leave enough time before the first session for everyone to receive the workbook and to prepare for Session 1.)

That's the plan. The material for study is here. All that is left is to add the most important ingredient: you and your responses to the call of God's Spirit. If you are open to the call, then you are ready for ministry both in the church and in the world. May this study help you and those with whom you gather to go deeper in your covenant to share in the ministry of God's people.

ASSIGNMENT FOR SESSION 1

1. Read and reflect on the focus statement for Session 1. Jot down insights or questions that occur to you as you consider various images of the church and what they suggest about your own calling to be in ministry.

2. Look through books, magazines, church library, Bible, hymnals, or worship bulletins for articles, quotes, pictures, or verses that present an image of the church, past or present. Bring these to Session 1.

3. Start a journal to keep track of your learnings. In the week prior to Session 1, spend at least thirty minutes thinking about the meaning of ministry. What does the concept of ministry suggest to you? How is ministry a part of your personal life and work? Name some of the ways your congregation is in ministry. On a separate sheet of paper write a few paragraphs about the practice and potential for ministry in your own life, congregation, and community.

4. As you prepare for this journey with the others in your group, reflect on the following passages. The first, from Richard Broholm, reminds us of Luther's conviction concerning the priesthood of all believers. The second, from *The COCU Consensus: In Quest of a Church Uniting,* is about baptism and ministry. Refer back to these statements several times in the week prior to Session 1 in order to focus your thoughts and prayers.

> Luther's conviction that all Christians are called to ministry challenges the Church every bit as much today as it did in 1517, when he posted his ninety-five theses. Today our current practices in the Church come uncomfortably close to a pre-Reformation understanding of "call," in which we think of clergy and missionaries as having the highest call.[1]

> All persons are called by their baptism and membership in the Church to manifest and bear witness to Christ's presence in the world in all their activities. Through their baptism, lay persons are called into the ministry of Jesus Christ. . . . Persons who are subsequently ordained continue to bear responsibility for the ministry common to all Christians to which they were called at their baptism.[2]

SESSION 1
IMAGES OF OUR CALLING

Objectives
- To introduce several biblical images of the church
- To consider the nature of ministry and "calling"
- To preview some key issues

Materials needed

Arts and crafts supplies, magazine pictures, etc., for making collages; copies of *The United Methodist Hymnal.*

FOCUS STATEMENT

Throughout the Old and New Testaments many different images are used to express the identity of the people of God, the community formed in response to God's initiative. The Hebrews were called "Israel," "the covenant people," "the chosen ones." The newly developing Christian community, in the first three centuries after Jesus, picked up some of these images and added others—describing its life together as "the Body of Christ," "the Servant People," and "the Vine and the Branches." Like the ancient Hebrews, the early church had to confirm its identity in the midst of suffering, up against an often hostile prevailing culture.

All images and metaphors of the church attempt to name in some way who the people of God are and what our relationship is to the living God. Like the Holy One we worship, our identity as a people has many dimensions. We are a community as dynamic and fluid as the One who answered Moses' question about God's name by saying: "I Am Who I Am" or "I will be who I will be" (Exodus 3:14). As a consequence, our ministry as the people of God is also "fluid," dynamic, and open to the future of God's calling and purpose for our lives in the church and in the world.

The Call to Ministry

Often when we think of the church, we think of the church building. Similarly, when we think of ministry, we think of the clergy. "A minister," we say, "is someone who is ordained to carry out the services of the church." As a result we may also think of the "call to ministry" as something that applies only to the clergy. These popular notions, however, miss the mark of our shared calling as the people of God in ministry. They miss the open and dynamic sense of what ministry can be when *all* of God's people follow the leading of the Spirit in the congregation and in the world.

In the Old Testament, the call to serve God came in a special way to certain individuals. For example, one might be called to be a prophet, a priest, or a king. Such a calling set a person apart from everyone else. Moreover, such callings required special credentials—a special command in the Law of Moses or a special inspiration of the Spirit.

Thus, to serve as a priest, like Aaron, one had to be born in the tribe of Levi. To serve as king, like Saul, one had to be recognized, selected, and duly anointed. And to speak the word of God as a prophet, like Isaiah, required a special visitation of the Spirit—a visitation that the average Israelite simply did not have or expect.

One of the great promises of the Old Testament, however, was that a time would come when God would pour out the Spirit "on all flesh; your sons and your daughters shall prophesy, your old men shall dream dreams, and your young men shall see visions. Even on the male and female slaves, in those days, I will pour out my spirit" (Joel 2:28-29).

In the New Testament, the followers of Jesus claimed that this promise was being fulfilled in their midst. On the day of Pentecost, according to the Book of Acts, Peter quoted the passage from Joel in order to explain how the ordinary disciples of Galilee were able to declare the good news about Jesus in a variety of languages (Acts 2:16-21). The explosion of the Spirit's power at Pentecost gave Christians courage to claim the Old Testament promises in ever broader ways. Images once applied only to Israel or to individuals within Israel now became the common calling of the Christian community: "But you are a chosen race, a royal priesthood, a holy nation, God's own people, in order that you may proclaim the mighty acts of him who called you out of darkness into his marvelous light" (1 Peter 2:9).

This biblical background runs against the popular notion of ministry that limits calling to the ordained clergy. According to the promise of the Old Testament and the witness of the New, the Spirit of God has been poured out upon all of God's people that we together may carry out the work of ministry in the church and in the world. But does this mean that all Christians are called to be "pastors" or to do "pastoral" type things—such as preaching and administering the sacraments? What does it really mean to affirm that all of God's people are called to ministry?

Images of Our Calling

The answer to that question will take several sessions to explore. A number of important issues lie hidden in the question itself. What are the gifts of the Spirit, and how do they relate to different ministries? How does the call to ministry connect with work, society, and life in the everyday world? What range of gifts for ministry does a congregation need in order to grow toward wholeness in Christ? Our approach to these questions will focus on three key biblical images of the church.

One result of affirming the general ministry of all Christians today will be a growing awareness that the gifts of the Spirit are many and varied. This was certainly the vision of the Apostle Paul when he spoke of the church as the *Body of Christ* (1 Corinthians 12). Too often we have equated ministry only with "pastoral" gifts. For Paul, the Body of Christ includes a special place for pastoral gifts; yet the gifts of the Spirit are diverse. To celebrate the full range of gifts in the Body of Christ is just as challenging today as it was in Paul's day. In order to move beyond the common stereotypes of ministry, we need to recover something of Paul's insistence on the variety and diversity of gifts in the Body of Christ. This will be our special focus in Session 2.

Another result of claiming our shared calling in ministry is the discovery that ministry touches the whole of life. Ministry is not just for church. Nor is it merely a "religious" or a "spiritual" matter. On the eve of the Passover festival, when the disciples were arguing about who was more spiritual, Jesus took upon himself the role of a common *servant,* He washed the disciples' feet in order to bring their aspirations for ministry back down to earth (John 13:1-17). Jesus' example is an invitation to us as well—to see an opportunity for ministry in every form of service; to be the church in the world; and to serve God in the practical round of work, society, and daily life. This will be our special focus in Session 3.

Yet another result of sharing in the ministry of God's people is a commitment to grow with others in the open and dynamic challenge of ministry itself. Jesus used the image of the *vine and the branches* to teach his disciples to "remain" in him if they hoped to do anything for the kingdom of God (John 15:1-5). Life and ministry in Christ is like a living plant. People grow. Gifts and callings do not stand still. Needs change. So do the possibilities for ministry. Growth also means stretching and learning to minister in new ways with people whose gifts balance our own. Like branches on a vine, we need connection with our source, and with each other, in order to grow and prosper in ministry. This is the focus of Session 4.

One of the most exciting things that can ever happen in a congregation is for the members to discover a renewed sense of their calling in ministry—both their general calling and their personal callings. Whenever and wherever in history the church has "come alive," this sense of calling has been part of the picture. Body of Christ, Servant of God, Vine and Branches: These are the images we will use to explore the call. They are not the only images that pertain to ministry, nor are they necessarily the most important. They do, however, lead us into some of the most important issues. Each image will help us to disclose part of what it means to affirm the ministry of God's people.

DISCUSSION AND DIALOGUE

1. Invite members of the group to introduce themselves to one another and to share why they are interested in this study.
   (*Note to Leader:* After completing this first round of sharing, you may wish to have only a few participants share in answering the following questions. Judge your time limitations and plan accordingly.)

2. Share your responses to the reading and reflection assignment for this session. What questions, issues, or new insights arose for the members of the group as a result of reading, reflecting, and journaling?

3. Spend a few minutes recalling images of the church that have been shared so far in this study. Invite group members to share other images that have been meaningful to them. Which image best describes your congregation? Which image best describes your own participation in ministry?

4. The United Methodist Church speaks of its ordained and diaconal ministers as carrying out "representative ministry." What does this mean to you?

5. As a way of bringing your discussion together, ask each participant to make a collage. Use the materials brought into the session and those provided by the leader to create a collage showing an image of the church that is important to you or one that represents your congregation at the present time. (If time permits, ask participants to share the meanings of their collages with each other.)

6. Finally, celebrate and anticipate what you are learning by means of the following worship service.

WORSHIP

O GOD, WE HEAR YOUR CALL

Begin by decorating the worship space with the collages you have created. Use symbols of the various images as part of the worship center. (You may also want to save these collages for use again in each of the other sessions.)

Hymn #550   "Christ, from Whom All Blessings Flow"
                               (stanzas 1, 2, and 3)

Litany of the Body of Christ:

Leader:	We are the Body of Christ.
People:	Joined together as a holy nation, a royal priesthood, God's own people.
Leader:	Set free in Christ, we are nevertheless called to service.
People:	But our service demands solidarity with others, true partnership to participate in God's ongoing creation.
Leader:	In partnership with God and with each other, we are called into community.
People:	*Gathered for the praise and glory of God; Scattered to be seeds of healing and reconciliation; and graced with God's steadfast love in all that we do and are.*
All:	AMEN.

Hymn #432   "Jesu, Jesu"

Prayer for Discernment (*in unison*):
    Grant us, O Lord, to know what is worth knowing,
    to love what is worth loving,
    to praise what delights you most,
    to hate what is offensive to you.
    Do not let us judge by what we see,
    or pass sentence according to what we hear,
    but to judge rightly between things that differ,
    and above all to search out and to do what pleases you,
    through Jesus Christ our Lord.
                         (adapted from Thomas à Kempis)[3]

Silence (3 minutes)

Hymn #558   "We Are the Church"
  (See the Appendix on page 47 for other hymn suggestions.)

ASSIGNMENT FOR SESSION 2

1. Read and reflect on the focus statement for Session 2. Jot down insights or questions that occur to you as you consider different kinds of spiritual gifts, their uses, and how they may be discovered.

2. Think about the ways you have experienced being in ministry. Whom did you serve? What was the nature of your ministry? What gift did you use in this ministry?

3. Conduct an informal interview with a co-worker or another member of the congregation. Use the following questions to discuss your understanding of spiritual gifts with each other.

   • What are your greatest natural talents and abilities?

   • Do you believe that God's Spirit has given you any special gifts for ministry? What are these?

   • How has God called you to use your natural talents and spiritual gifts?

   • Have your gifts been recognized and affirmed by the congregation and/or the community? How?

4. In your journal, choose one of the following scriptural passages on spiritual gifts, and record your reflections in words or images:

   Romans 12:1-8
   1 Corinthians 12:4-26
   2 Peter 4:7-11

SESSION 2
CALLED AND GIFTED

Objectives
- To affirm the ministry of all Christians
- To consider the variety of spiritual gifts
- To explore your own sense of giftedness for ministry

Materials needed
Workbooks, journals, interview notes, hymnals

FOCUS STATEMENT

In his first letter to the Christians at Corinth, the Apostle Paul described the church as the *Body of Christ*. Paul's letter shows that the Corinthian congregation had many needs and many different possibilities for ministry—both in the congregation and in the city of Corinth. The Corinthian Christians, however, were at odds with each other. They argued about which gifts and ministries should be regarded as most important (12:20-26). Paul did not take sides in this debate. He refused to exalt one gift at the expense of another. Rather, using the image of the Body of Christ, he charged the Corinthian Christians to discover and to celebrate their diversity.

The Variety of Spiritual Gifts

Paul explained the diversity of the Body of Christ in terms of a variety of spiritual gifts. According to Paul, every member of the Body of Christ is given some "manifestation of the Spirit for the common good" (1 Corinthians 12:7). In Session 4 we shall look at the unifying purpose of the gifts. In this session our focus is diversity.

In the letter to Corinth, Paul gave names to at least thirteen different gifts: wisdom, knowledge, faith, healing, working miracles, prophecy, discernment of spirits, speaking in tongues, interpretation of tongues, apostleship, teaching, forms of assistance, and leadership (1 Corinthians 12:8-10, 28). In his letters to Rome and to Ephesus, Paul mentioned some of these same gifts and added a few others: exhortation, generosity, compassion (Romans 12:8), evangelism, and pastoring (Ephesians 4:11).

It is not always possible to tell from Paul's lists where one gift stops and another starts. Are the "deeds of power" in 1 Corinthians 12:28 the same thing or something different from the "working of miracles" mentioned in verse 10? Likewise, are the "forms of assistance" in 1 Corinthians 12:28 the same as or different from the gifts of "generosity" and "compassion" in Romans 12:8?

Perhaps it is a mistake to try to force too much precision on Paul's lists. After all, Paul himself did not leave just one list. His emphasis with the Corinthians was not upon providing a comprehensive or detailed description of every gift. Rather, he spoke of *"varieties* of gifts . . . *varieties* of services . . . *varieties* of activities" (1 Corinthians 12:4-6). In this way, his lists may well have been designed more to suggest than to exhaust the different kinds of gifts.

The suggestive style of Paul's lists, however, does not diminish the special character of particular gifts. Even if Paul did not intend to name every gift, the fact remains that he did name some. Some of the gifts he named, moreover, imply the use of very different kinds of skills. One of the most helpful summaries in this regard is given by Charles V. Bryant in *Rediscovering the Charismata.* Following Bryant we can think of the gifts in four broad groupings:

> *Speaking* gifts include exhortation, wisdom, knowledge, tongues, prophecy, and teaching.
>
> *Serving* gifts include forms of assistance, leadership, generosity, and compassion.
>
> *Sustaining* gifts include pastoring, apostleship, evangelism, and faith.
>
> *Sign* gifts include healing, tongues, interpretation of tongues, miracles, and discernment of spirits.[4]

The Gifts of the Spirit Today

Congregations today have many different experiences of the gifts of the Spirit. Some congregations seem to "specialize" in certain kinds of gifts—sign gifts, for example, or serving gifts. Other congregations seem hard-pressed to move beyond the particular sustaining gifts of the pastor. Few congregations show the full variety and diversity that Paul recommended. What would it be like today if all congregations were able to discover all of their spiritual gifts and to live more completely as the Body of Christ?

One result of living more completely as the Body of Christ today would surely be the eradication of the notion that "ministry" is the work of the professional clergy alone. Paul certainly recognized a special role for those gifts that we often associate with the ordained ministry—for example, starting churches (apostleship), preaching, and teaching. But he set these alongside the other gifts, not in place of them (1 Corinthians 12:28).

One thing we can do to catch up with Paul on this point is to change the way we speak about ministry. Instead of using the word *minister* to refer to ordained persons, we might speak of the clergy as "pastors" or "teachers," and extend the title of *minister* to all. From this standpoint, every congregation may have one or more pastors, and every member is a minister.

Another result of embracing our life together as the Body of Christ will be a growing awareness that the gifts of the Spirit are many and varied—as many as the people whom the Spirit calls and as varied as the occasions that give rise to ministry. We need to think creatively about different gifts in order to see their full potential both for laity and for clergy.

Gifts of speaking, for example, are needed in many different ways. Words of exhortation, wisdom, and knowledge are needed not only in worship services or prayer group meetings, but also in personal relationships, in meetings to discuss budget priorities, and in groups that gather to serve. Such gifts can also come into play in community meetings and public hearings, where issues of public policy and civic duty are hammered out. In all of these settings, the gifts can be given by the Spirit through clergy and laity alike. We need to become more sensitive to the presence of such gifts in our midst. We need to call upon such gifts as a regular part of our life together.

Yet another result of living more completely as the Body of Christ will be a commitment to bridge the gap between church and world. Spiritual gifts are not just for a "spiritual" or "religious" part of life. Consider the sign gift of healing, for example. This gift is not just for extraordinary circumstances of sickness and conflict, but also for our daily life of caring and sharing. The physician's art can also be a gift of ministry. In many cases, our ideas about particular gifts simply need to be expanded in order to include the full range of opportunities for service in the world. (This will be our special focus in the next session.)

Discovering Your Gifts

Gifts discovery can be a wonderful and creative process. Imagine your congregation as each member discovers a very personal sense of contribution in ministry. Imagine the empowerment as the gifts and ministries are named. Picture all those whose lives are touched by ministries that flourish—both in the congregation and in the surrounding community.

But how does a congregation go about discovering the gifts of its members for ministry? We shall be working on this question in each of the sessions that follow. At this point, we can begin by reviewing a few basic principles.

One of the best places to begin the assessment of gifts for ministry is with the evidence of natural talent. Persons who enjoy talking to groups may have a natural talent for one or more of the speaking gifts. A person who struggles with stage fright, on the other hand, may invite unnecessary anxiety by aspiring to such gifts. Likewise, the gift of administration implies a knack for organizational details. Some people seem almost born to such tasks; others do not.

To be sure, evidence of natural talent is not a fail-safe guide. Natural talents are not necessarily the same as spiritual gifts. Indeed, when one submits a "natural" talent to the Spirit, the talent itself will often take on new meaning and move in new directions. Further, there are occasions where God's call requires precisely what our natural inclinations reject. We shall look at some of these issues again in Session 4. But natural talents do provide a sensible starting point for thinking about spiritual gifts.

Another solid starting point for thinking about spiritual gifts is obtaining the witness of the community. We do well to confirm claims of giftedness through the response of others—especially those who are *supposed* to be the recipients of the ministry offered through a gift. This, however, can work both ways. A person's readiness to use the gift of teaching may be either confirmed or called into question by the community's witness. On the other hand, members of the congregation may discern a gift where the gifted person has not previously recognized his or her own potential for ministry.

Another starting point for the discernment of gifts is with the ordinary needs that surround every congregation in daily life. One way to overcome the tendency to spiritualize the gifts is simply to open our eyes and ears to God's call in the ordinary—in the need for a cool drink of water or a merciful word. In such cases, the gifts we need to answer the call are no further away than our readiness to hear, to see, and to say, "Here am I; send me" (Isaiah 6:8).

In the final analysis, the only adequate starting place for our exploration of ministry as God's people is having the same confidence as Paul that Christ is the Lord of the church and that his Spirit can be trusted to lead us on our journey. What are your gifts for ministry? Where is the Spirit calling you? As you seek to respond, think creatively, be sensitive to one another, and remember Paul's teaching that there are many kinds of gifts and many kinds of service.

DISCUSSION AND DIALOGUE

1. Share your responses to the reading and reflection assignment
   for this session. What questions, issues, or new insights arose for
   the members of the group as a result of reading through the
   focus statement and the biblical passages on spiritual gifts?

2. Share the results of the gift and talent interviews conducted
   earlier in the week. (Leader's note: Use the following questions
   to guide discussion. Depending on the nature of your group,,
   there may not be time for everyone to respond to each question.
   Judge your time limitations and plan accordingly.)

   • In general, what did you learn from the interview? Were you
     and the person you interviewed comfortable with the discus-
     sion of spiritual gifts? Why or why not?

   • By what signs did you determine your sense of calling and
     giftedness for ministry? Did you usually regard your spiritual
     gifts and your natural talents as one and the same? Why or
     why not?

   • Do you feel that your community of faith has supported you in
     the identification and use of your spiritual gifts? How has this
     support been shown?

3. Now, help each other explore more fully your sense of calling
   and giftedness. (Leader's note: Be prepared to lead the group in
   the following exercise. Work in groups of three or four persons
   and discuss the following questions.)

   • When I look at my congregation and community, what oppor-
     tunities do I see that seem to call for ministry? What gifts are
     needed to meet these opportunities?

   • What natural talents and spiritual gifts do I have? Are my gifts
     more on the order of speaking, serving, sustaining, or sign
     gifts? How can these gifts contribute to a special area of
     ministry?

- Recall one way you have experienced being in ministry during the last year. Were you sustained in this ministry by others? How? By whom?

- What can we do in our congregation to foster a greater sense of the ministry of all Christians in the Body of Christ?

4. Finally, celebrate your learnings thus far by means of the service of worship on p. 16.

WORSHIP

PRAISE THE GIVER OF THE GIFTS

(If you have symbols of the Body of Christ from Session 1, place these prominently in your worship space.)

Hymn #550   "Christ, from Whom All Blessings Flow"

Scripture:
  First Reader: 1 Corinthians 12:1-11
  Second Reader: 1 Corinthians 12:12-19

Prayer (*in unison*):
          Dear God,
          Make me a willing discoverer
          of the gifts you have placed within each of us.
          Teach me to rejoice
          in the beauty you have planted within me.
          Cleanse the dirt from my inward eyes
          that I might see the grace showered on all.
          Help me truly to rejoice
          in the richness of your love. Amen.
                                        Keith S. Karlile[5]

Hymn #114   "Many Gifts, One Spirit"

Litany of the Gifted

  Leader: Listen one and all! We are involved in God's work.

  People: What can I possibly do for God?

  Leader: Whatever you do in word or deed, do all in the
                 name of Jesus Christ.

  People: Everything? What about yard work and shopping
                 for groceries?

  Leader: Do all in the name of Jesus Christ.

  People: Does that apply to all my jobs?

  Leader: Do all in the name of Jesus Christ.

People:	Sure it counts when I go to church or teach Sunday school, but what about going camping or to the park with my family?
Leader:	Do all in the name of Jesus Christ.
People:	Is that all there is to it? Are you sure there is not more?
Leader:	Do all in the name of Jesus Christ, giving thanks to God the Father through him.
All:	Whatever you do in word or deed, do all in the name of Jesus Christ, giving thanks to God the Father through him. Amen.[6]
Hymn #712	"I Sing a Song of the Saints of God"

ASSIGNMENT FOR SESSION 3

1. Read and reflect on the focus statement for Session 3. Jot down insights or questions that occur to you as you think about different kinds of service and how they relate to the ministry of the church.

2. In the course of the coming week, think about the different kinds of service that you encounter in your places of work, leisure, and other activities. Describe these forms of service in the framework of the following questions:

> Who is serving?
>
> Who is being served?
>
> What is being done?
>
> Where does the service take place?
>
> When does the service take place?
>
> Why is the service being provided?
>
> Is this a form of service that qualifies as "ministry"? Why or why not?

3. In your journal for the coming week, meditate on one of the following scripture passages and record your reflections in words or images.

> Luke 4:16-21   Acts 3:1-10   Matthew 18:1-5

4. Also, consider the following statements from Stanley Menking and from Archbishop Oscar Romero, as you think about ministry in relation to serving others.

> . . . the original human vocation from God had to do with caring for God's creation and working with God so creation might reach its divine goal. The coming of Christ did not set aside that vocation. Therefore, as laity go about all of their responsibilities, in all of their life, they are about the mission that was given to everyone when they were created *imago dei.* . . . [7]

I repeat what I told you once before when we feared we might be left without a radio station: God's best microphone is the church, and the church is all of you. Let each one of you, in your own job, your own vocation—nun, married person, bishop, priest, high-school or university student, workman, laborer, market woman—each one in your own place live the faith intensely and feel that in your surroundings you are a true microphone of God our Lord.[8]

SESSION 3
CALLED TO BE SERVANTS

Objectives
- To affirm the connection between ministry and service
- To consider Jesus' example as the Servant of God
- To think creatively about how our own lives and labors involve opportunities for serving God in the church and in the world

Materials needed
Stationery and pens for epistle writing, copies of the United Methodist *Discipline*, hymnals

FOCUS STATEMENT

At a church camp one summer, the youth were encouraged to consider their sense of being called to be about God's work. During the closing campfire, all were given the opportunity to share their calling with the group and to light a candle symbolizing their commitment to respond to that call.

One young man had sensed during his high school years that God wanted him to become a public schoolteacher working in the inner city. So he considered this during the week, prayed about it, and, during the closing ceremony, was prepared to accept this call and commit himself to respond.

As the ceremony unfolded, various persons went forward and whispered in the leader's ear. First it was announced, "David has been called to full-time Christian service as a pastor," then, "Joan has been called to full-time Christian service as a missionary nurse," and so on.

The young man approached the leader and whispered, "God has called me to serve as a high school teacher in the inner city." Quietly the leader responded, "Oh, no, you must have misunderstood. This is just for those who have been called to full-time Christian service."

It took forty years for the now grown man to share the experience and feel his call had been heard, accepted, and affirmed. In between the two experiences, he had been faithful on the "front lines" of Christian service, living his discipleship in his work as a teacher—inspiring, encouraging, disciplining, persevering.[9]

Jesus, the Servant of God

On the evening of the Passover meal, according to the Gospel of John, Jesus took a towel and a bowl of water and began to wash his disciples' feet (John 13:1-5). When he had finished, he explained to them:

> You call me Teacher and Lord—and you are right, for that is what I am. So if I, your Lord and Teacher, have washed your feet, you also ought to wash one another's feet. For I have set you an example, that you also should do as I have done to you. Very truly, I tell you, servants are not greater than their master, nor are messengers greater than the one who sent them. If you know these things, you are blessed if you do them (John 13:13-17).

Jesus' act was an act of common service. Indeed, in a land of dusty roads and sandals, washing feet was a daily act of personal cleanliness. In a well-to-do house, the job might fall to a household servant. Among the poor, it could become an act of hospitality.

On the evening of the Passover, the disciples had forgotten to extend the common courtesies to one another. According to the Gospel of Luke, they would argue later among themselves "as to which one of them was to be regarded as the greatest" (Luke 22:24). In this setting Jesus took a towel and began to wash their feet.

When Jesus embraced the role of the servant as a model of God's work among the people, he went against some commonly held expectations of his day. Many people in Jesus' day knew of Isaiah's prophesies concerning a servant who would "be as a light to the nations" (Isaiah 49:6) and who would be "wounded for our trans-

gressions" (53:5). But few expected that the prophet's words would
be fulfilled through deeds of common service among the people of
the land.

Servanthood Today

Jesus' model of service is just as challenging today as it was in the
early years of his ministry. For one thing, the servant model challenges us to recognize the potential for service in every kind of
ministry. All too often the church has been captured by the view
that certain callings are inherently more important than others. In
ministry, however, there are no "little" people and no insignificant
callings.

Jesus' model of service has a "leveling" influence on the practice
of ministry in general. The basic Greek word for ministry is
diakonia, i.e., service. When the Apostle Paul wanted to describe
the gifts of ministry in general, he spoke of "varieties of service"
(1 Corinthians 12:5). From the standpoint of service, every ministry
is equal. Though we can speak as we did in the last chapter of the
differences between special gifts, we can also speak of every gift as a
way of serving. When someone teaches, helps, shows compassion,
or prays for healing, these are ways of serving. But so too does the
preacher serve by preaching and the leader by leading. This does
not diminish the uniqueness of each gift, but it does bring out the
common purpose of all gifts in the image of Christ.

Likewise, Jesus' model of service also challenges us to recognize
the potential for ministry in every kind of service "in the world."
Even after we affirm the connectedness of all ministry through
serving, we may still think of ministry as something that happens
primarily "at the church building." Jesus' act of footwashing, for
instance, was not a "religious" office. Rather, in the society of the
ancient world, it was a matter of common everyday courtesy. Thus,
his example calls us to open our eyes to the full possibilities for
serving God *in the world.*

Jesus responded to many kinds of human needs. He not only
washed feet; he also fed people, healed them, and interceded for
them with the public authorities. In the Gospel of Matthew, he laid
down an ultimate test of faithful discipleship—not religious devotion per se, or public acclaim, but caring for "the least of these."

Such service, Jesus said, even if it goes unrecognized, is truly service to him (Matthew 25:31-46).

Serving God in the world, however, must never be confused with subordination or domination. For some, the call to "service" has been only a thin disguise for a harsh reality of indignity and injustice. Third world people, minority groups, and women have drawn special attention to this problem. Jesus' model of service was one of partnership in ministry, not of domination. Jesus did not seek to dominate his disciples. Rather, he worked to liberate them from the need to dominate (or to be dominated) in order to free them for service with him and with each other.

Ministry that is centered in service aims at the empowerment of those who are served. Whether you are a pastor or a business professional, a cook or an evangelist, one test of your ministry will be its capacity to release, to receive, and to rejoice in the contributions of those you serve. As Letty Russell has written:

> Set free in Christ, we are nevertheless called to service of our neighbor, and it is out of this empowerment for service that partnerships happen. . . . There is no service without partnership, from the perspective of the Christian faith. God serves because God has chosen to be our covenant partner. We serve because God has served us and made us partners with all humanity. Genuine service involves solidarity with those being served and a willingness to be served as well as to serve.[10]

In this light, every job, every occupation, every contribution to the improvement of life can become an occasion for ministry. The possibilities for service are endless—in the home, through volunteer work, in many different kinds of occupations, such as farmer, grocer, lawyer, tailor, builder, banker, garbage collector, doctor, bus driver. Every job, every kindness, every labor of love in public or private life can become a form of ministry. Such a prospect invites us once again to think broadly and creatively about the meaning and practice of the spiritual gifts.

DISCUSSION AND DIALOGUE

1. Share your responses to the reading and reflection assignment
   for this session. What questions, issues, or new insights arose for
   the members of the group as a result of reading the focus
   statement and thinking about the possibilities for service in the
   world?

2. Divide into three groups and have each group read one of the
   following passages:

   Matthew 25:31-46   Luke 10:25-37   Acts 2

   In the groups, discuss how these passages relate to being the
   scattered church, serving and transforming the world. Let each
   group or team make a brief report about its passage to the
   others.

3. In pairs, look through the section on "Social Principles" in *The
   Book of Discipline* of The United Methodist Church. Ask part-
   ners to describe at least one area where they feel called to
   cultivate a way of serving in the world. Invite them to think
   concretely about the "who, what, when, where, and why" of
   serving and to share this with each other.

4. Now ask each person to write an epistle to his or her partner,
   giving advice and encouragement for ministries of service in the
   world.

5. Now celebrate your learnings together by means of the following worship service.

WORSHIP

PRAISE THE GOD WHO SERVES

(If you have symbols of the servant image from Session 1, locate these prominently in your worship space.)

Hymn #712   "I Sing a Song of the Saints of God"

Prayer of Mutual Encouragement:

Left:	I'm not here to judge you; I'm here to listen to what you need to say.
Right:	I'm not here to blame you; I'm here to know how you feel.
Left:	I'm not here to say, "It shouldn't have been this way"; I'm here to share your questions.
Right:	So though I do not know how best to ease your load; I'm here so you don't feel alone.
Left:	I'm not here to offer answers to rights or wrongs, or to question anything.
Right:	But I'm here to simply be with you when things are not as you'd wish they were.
All:	I am your friend. And I care.[11]

Hymn #432   "Jesu, Jesu"

Sharing of the Epistles

Prayer for Courage to Do Justice (*unison*):

O Lord,
open my eyes that I may see the needs of others;
open my ears that I may hear their cries;
open my heart so that they need not be without succor;
let me not be afraid to defend the weak
because of the anger of the strong,
nor afraid to defend the poor
because of the anger of the rich.
Show me where love and hope and faith are needed,
and use me to bring them to those places.
And so open my eyes and my ears

that I may this coming day be able
to do some work of peace for thee. Amen.[12]

Hymn #413   "A Charge to Keep I Have"

ASSIGNMENT FOR SESSION 4

1. Read and reflect on the focus statement for Session 4. Jot down insights or questions that occur to you as you think about what it means to grow in grace as you serve in ministry.

2. In the course of the week, find and read materials on the Methodist revival in England, the early American religious revival, or the explosive growth of the Christian church in Asia, Africa, and Latin America today. Note any features of these religious movements that seem different from your own experience of "church." (NOTE: If you do not have a church library, ask your pastor for help in finding sources. Public libraries may also be able to help. Leaders could compile in advance a brief list of locally available resources.)

3. In your journal for the coming week, meditate on one of the following passages and record your reflections in words or images.

    Ephesians 4:7-13   Hebrews 10:23-25

4. Also, consider the following statement on the church (from *The Book of Discipline* of The United Methodist Church) and the quote from John Wesley outlining his hopes for his Methodist followers. Record some of your own thoughts and hopes for the church today.

> A local church is a community of true believers under the Lordship of Christ. It is the redemptive fellowship in which the Word of God is preached by persons divinely called, and the Sacraments are duly administered according to Christ's own appointment. Under the discipline of the Holy Spirit the Church exists for the maintenance of worship, the edification of believers, and the redemption of the world (¶201).[13]
>
> I am not afraid that the people called Methodists should ever cease to exist either in Europe or America. But I am afraid, lest they should only exist as a dead sect, having the form of religion without the

power. And this undoubtedly will be the case, unless
they hold fast both the doctrine, spirit and discipline
with which they first set out.

John Wesley[14]

SESSION 4
CALLED TO GROW IN GRACE

Objectives
- To affirm the goal of growth in ministry
- To examine some means and patterns of growth
- To consider what growth implies for the future of ministry in your own life and congregation

Materials needed
Wide ribbon, markers, hymnals

FOCUS STATEMENT

As Jesus neared the climactic events of his ministry, he gathered his disciples around him and gave them instructions for the future. On one occasion, Jesus put special emphasis on the disciples' need to "abide in him." He used the image of the "vine and the branches" to make his point clear.

> I am the true vine, and my Father is the vinegrower. He removes every branch in me that bears no fruit. Every branch that bears fruit he prunes to make it bear more fruit. . . . Abide in me as I abide in you. Just as the branch cannot bear fruit by itself unless it abides in the vine, neither can you unless you abide in me. I am the vine, you are the branches. Those who abide in me and I in them bear much fruit, because apart from me you can do nothing (John 15:1-5).

Jesus' words challenged his first disciples with two distinct but related goals: "Abide in me" and "bear much fruit." In order to accept this challenge today, we need to consider both what it

29

means to abide in Christ and how this gives rise to bearing fruit in the Christian life and in the Christian community.

Abiding in Christ

What does it really mean to abide in Christ? How do we do this? Is this the same thing as bearing fruit?

From the earliest times, Christians have understood that our life together in Christ is sustained through the "means of grace" which Jesus ordained. Jesus gave his first disciples many lessons in how to abide in the grace of God. We recall how he taught his disciples to pray. In his "high priestly prayer" (John 17), he called on the power of prayer to strengthen his disciples and to assure them of his continuing presence with them, even after his death. But Jesus also told his disciples to serve him in "the least of these" (Matthew 25:45), to preach the good news to all nations (Acts 2:7; Matthew 28:19-20), and to remember him in the sharing of a common meal (Mark 14:22-25; 1 Corinthians 11:24-26).

From this beginning, the means of grace have always been a key for the church of what it means to abide in Christ. In the Acts of the Apostles, Luke described the life of the early Christian community: "They devoted themselves to the apostles' teaching and fellowship, to the breaking of bread and the prayers" (Acts 2:42). According to Luke, they also "had all things in common; they would sell their possessions and goods and distribute the proceeds to all, as any had need" (Acts 2:44-45). Do you hear the echoes of Jesus' teaching?

The means of grace, according to the teaching of John Wesley, are those practices and sacraments—ordained in scripture and proven in experience—whereby we "put ourselves in the way" of God's gracious love and action toward us. Under this general heading Wesley included both the "instituted" means of grace—such as prayer, scripture reading, preaching, the Lord's Supper—and the "prudential" means of grace—such as doing various specific acts of mercy, justice, and compassion in service to others. In all of these ways, through all of these means, according to Wesley, the Spirit of Christ is ready to meet us and to transform our lives through the power of grace.

At this point we should also notice an important connection between the means of grace and the gifts of the Spirit. To put things boldly, the means of grace depend on the operation of specific gifts. If listening to the scripture is a means of grace, preaching and teaching are gifts of the Spirit. If deeds of mercy and compassion are means of grace, the gifts of compassion and generosity are examples for the whole congregation. If prayer is a means of grace, those with gifts of knowledge, wisdom, tongues, and interpretation may enhance the prayer life of the whole community. Gifts of ministry, like means of grace, are given that we may abide in Christ and bear much fruit.

If this is what it means to abide in Christ, however, what does it mean to bear much fruit? How is bearing fruit related to abiding in Christ?

Bearing Fruit

When we speak of "bearing fruit," a number of things may come to mind. We may think, for example, of "winning others to Christ" through evangelism. Jesus himself spoke of how the "fields are ripe for harvesting" (John 4:35). On the other hand, we may think with the Apostle Paul of the fruits of the Spirit—love, joy, peace, patience, etc. (Galatians 5:22)—and how these are signs of a healthy Christian life. Jesus said that "each tree is known by its own fruit" (Luke 6:44). Or we may think of how the goal of all ministry, according to another of Paul's letters, is to build up the Body of Christ in love (Ephesians 4:11-16).

In all of these meanings, however, it is important to keep one thing perfectly clear. Bearing fruit is a process of growth and change. It is not a matter of finding a secure or comfortable place in which to stop growing or changing. This is clear from Jesus' own illustration: Those who abide in him and bear fruit will experience "pruning," to the end that they may bear more fruit. Abiding in Christ and bearing fruit always involves growth and change.

This suggests a very dynamic connection between abiding in Christ (the means of grace, the gifts of the Spirit) and bearing the fruits of Christian life. To abide in Christ and to grow as disciples we need the means of grace and the gifts of the Spirit. In this sense our growth is dependent on the grace that God conveys to us through each other. And our gifts and ministries are not an end in themselves. They have a greater goal in God's purpose for all.

Vine and Branches Today

When we think of ministry as a dynamic, living process, in cooperation with others whose gifts serve, complement, and even balance our own, we must also be prepared for some surprises. Jesus' image of the vine and the branches calls us forward into an open adventure of mutual growth and ministry.

The ministry of God's people holds many promises. It also holds many challenges. We know, for example, that the use of the means of grace can become a dry and lifeless routine. John Wesley understood this when he warned his early Methodist followers never to confuse the means of grace with the end for which grace is given—love. To confuse the means of grace with the end of grace would be to risk turning ministry into a formalistic affair—a program for institutional maintenance—rather than a matter of heart and life and genuine connection with God and other people.

We need to remember that the early Methodist sense of calling was to be a renewal movement within their own "denomination," the Church of England. Like them, we need to stir up the gifts that are among us and in us—clergy and laity alike—in order to stay awake and alive to the grace that God conveys to all every day. After a six-month stay in Latin America, noted author and scholar Henri Nouwen summed up his learnings in this way:

> I learned what I must have forgotten somewhere in my busy, well-planned, and very "useful" life. I learned that everything that is, is freely given by the God of love. All is grace. Light and water, shelter and food, work and free time, children, parents and grandparents, birth and death—it is all given to us. Why? So that we can say *gracias,* thanks: thanks to God, thanks to each other, thanks to all and everyone.[15]

Once again, we need to remember that the gifts of the Spirit and the means of grace are not an end in themselves. Biblical students have long noted that Paul's famous chapter on love (1 Corinthians 13) follows immediately on his discussion of the spiritual gifts. For Paul, the ultimate purpose of the gifts was not to bolster an individual's prestige or reputation—though Paul clearly affirmed a sense of calm self-esteem that comes with knowing that we are gifted by God (Romans 12:3). The ultimate purpose of the gifts is to build up the Body of Christ in love.

The simple fact is, in order to abide in Christ, we need one another, the means of grace, and the gifts that the Spirit gives to all. Christ is the vine. We are the branches. Our lives and ministries grow together with each other as we receive and share the grace provided through each.

Finally, we should also acknowledge that the discovery of gifts for ministry can be a very stretching process. In keeping with John Wesley's covenant prayer, sometimes our sense of calling will match what we perceive as our natural gifts and personality, and sometimes it will not. For example, we may not feel comfortable speaking in public, yet God calls us to witness by sharing our faith story with the congregation, or by being part of a public hearing on community residences for mentally ill persons. We may like leading groups in planning or action, but God calls us to a ministry of listening through a suicide hotline.

In this light it would be a mistake to consider a particular spiritual gift as the end of one's growth and potential for ministry. The Spirit calls us to a process of ongoing discovery—in our personal lives, in our congregations, and in our world.

If we think of ministry as a life process, we must be open to the challenges, opportunities, and, yes, the surprises that the Spirit brings. This may require being patient with others whose gifts we do not yet understand. It may even require being open to participate in areas of ministry for which we do not feel completely qualified. In any event it will involve the promise and the warning of abiding in Christ. In him we will bear much fruit. Apart from him we can do nothing.

DISCUSSION AND DIALOGUE

1. Share your responses to the reading and reflection assignment for this session. What questions, issues, or new insights have arisen for the members of the group as a result of reading through the focus statement and other materials on growing in grace?

2. Working in groups of three or four, ask participants to share their experiences of growth through the means of grace. Which of the means of grace have been most important in the lives of group members? How have people changed over time in their use of or response to the different means of grace? Have some means become more important and others less, as a result of life changes or sense of calling?

3. Using markers and pieces of ribbon, write some expression of grace you have received in a way you did not expect or through a person you would not have chosen.

4. Now celebrate your learnings together thus far by means of the following worship service.

WORSHIP

PRAISE THE GOD OF GRACE

(If you have symbols of the vine and branches from Session 1, locate these prominently in your worship space.)

Hymn #561 "Jesus, United by Thy Grace"

Scripture:

First Reader: Ephesians 4:7-13
Second Reader: Ephesians 4:14-16

Silence (three minutes)

Prayers of Thanksgiving:
Spontaneous prayers of thanks for the manifestations of God's grace and for the lives of those who minister.

Offering of Gifts:
Present an offering of gifts to God by processing with the ribbons and presenting them at the worship table.

Hymn #606 "Come, Let Us Use the Grace Divine"

Closing prayer (*in unison*):

Lord, make me an instrument of thy peace;
        where there is hatred, let me sow love;
        where there is injury, pardon;
        where there is doubt, faith;
        where there is despair, hope;
        where there is darkness, light;
        and where there is sadness, joy.
O Divine Master,
        grant that I may not so much seek
        to be consoled as to console;
        to be understood, as to understand;
        to be loved, as to love;
        for it is in giving that we receive,
        it is in pardoning that we are pardoned,
        and it is in dying that we are born to eternal life.

Saint Francis of Assisi[16]

ASSIGNMENT FOR SESSION 5

1. Read and reflect on the focus statement for Session 5. Jot down thoughts and feelings that arise as you consider the future of your calling in ministry—as an individual, with your congregation, or perhaps, with the members of this group.

2. Look back through the various words and images you have recorded in your journal throughout this study. Select one passage from each of the previous sessions in your journal (call, gifts, service, growth), and make some further notes about where you think you are growing and learning in ministry.

3. In your journal for the coming week, meditate on one of the following passages, and record your reflections in words or images.

Genesis 9:8-17   Genesis 12:1-3

Hebrews 10:15-23   1 Corinthians 11:23-26

4. Also use the following prayer from John Wesley's service for covenant renewal to focus your thoughts and prayers as we move toward the final week of our time together.

> I am no longer my own, but thine.
> Put me to what thou wilt, rank me with whom thou wilt.
> Put me to doing, put me to suffering.
> Let me be employed by thee or laid aside for thee,
> exalted for thee or brought low by thee.
> Let me be full, let me be empty.
> Let me have all things, let me have nothing.
> I freely and heartily yield all things
> to thy pleasure and disposal.
> And now, O gracious and blessed God,
> Father, Son, and Holy Spirit,
> thou art mine, and I am thine. So be it.
> And the covenant which I have made on earth,
> let it be ratified in heaven. Amen.
>
> *John Wesley*[17]

SESSION 5
CALLED TO COVENANT

Objectives
- To affirm our various callings to ministry
- To make a covenant with God and with each other concerning our continuing hopes for ministry
- To support one another through prayer and worship

Materials needed
Paper and pencils for covenant writing, index cards for writing prayer requests, advance preparations for worship (see page 40), hymnals

FOCUS STATEMENT

Throughout this study, we have discussed God's call to persons and how our response to that call results in our knowing "who and whose we are." Our identity and belonging are confirmed and fulfilled as part of a faith community that seeks to live out righteousness, compassion, prayer, and praise.

There is always a wholeness to the covenant between God and people. In community we are freed to be the persons we truly are. In living out God's vision of shalom, we are sustained by God's grace in and through community. As covenant people, we are in relationship with God and with each other. At the same time, God is in relationship with us and with the others in our community. Others in our community are in relationship with God and with us. The web that binds us together is the stuff through which God's creative, redeeming, and sustaining power is at work in our lives.

Covenant Writing

In each of the preceding sessions we have examined a particular facet of the calling of all Christians to be in ministry. In each case,

37

we have also considered how the issues apply to us as individuals and as congregations. As we move now toward a time of covenant for the future, with God and with each other, we begin by gathering together some of the earlier learnings.

COVENANT WRITING: Clause 1—During the second session, we examined a variety of gifts and ministries to which the members of the Body of Christ may be called. We also considered our own experiences of calling and ministry and some of the ways a community can encourage and confirm the gifts of its members. As part of your covenant with God, in the space below, write a description of at least one gift you think you may have and one area of need in your community where God may be calling you to use this gift. Refer to Session 2 as needed.

COVENANT WRITING: Clause 2—In Session 3, we discussed the call to the church and to individual Christians to serve as Christ served in the world, to be in partnership with others, and to stand in solidarity with oppressed and marginalized persons and groups. We saw how service has a leveling influence upon all ministries and how it opens a door to the broader meaning of ministry in the church and in the world. As you think about your life in the world of work and in other "public" activities—whether at home, at school, in an office, in a factory, on a farm, or in another setting— name at least two areas you would like to include in your covenant with God in response to the call to serve. Be specific. Refer to your reflections in Session 3 as needed.

COVENANT WRITING: Clause 3—In Session 4, we explored how the Spirit moves through the life of the covenant community and how the "means of grace" serve to sustain our life together. Apart from our connection with Christ and with one another, discovering gifts and even serving in the world can become empty activities. Our spiritual life is grounded in God's grace, Christ's redemptive love, and the power of the Holy Spirit. Among the means of grace related to devotion, worship, compassion, and justice, name those areas where you feel the greatest need for self-discipline or for greater openness to the gifts of your brothers and sisters, in order to deepen your own sense of mission and ministry.

One of the wonderful things about a covenant is that it is "relational." A covenant is designed for the relationship between two or more persons. The covenant to be in ministry is a covenant between you, God, and the whole community of faith. The process of moving through the sessions of this study has involved a covenant between you, God, and the members of this group. As your group comes to the close of this study, however, your covenants to be in ministry remain in full force. Consider, then, how you may continue "to stir one another up to love and good works."

DISCUSSION AND DIALOGUE

Leading up to a time of corporate worship, persons may write on cards their prayer requests related to the covenant clauses written earlier. Prayers could include asking for strength and courage to follow through in ministry, offering thanks for a clear sense of kind of and place for ministry, and asking for God's confirmation of one's sense of calling through others. This can be an open time of sharing and caring for one another and perhaps for covenanting together to carry on in ministry or in support of each other.

WORSHIP

Advance preparations for the closing covenant service:
- Arrange the room with a table and appropriate symbols. In addition to the symbols and images of the church which you created in Session 1, you may also want to use flowers, candles, seashells, etc.
- Have communion elements ready to be brought forward with offering of covenants.
- Assign persons as readers.
- Participants should be prepared to share significant learnings during the "witness" section.
- If not part of the study group, invite pastor(s) to share in the consecration and serving of elements of the Eucharist. (Ordained persons may take special responsibility for the prayers of consecration on page 44.)

COVENANT SERVICE

(This version of John Wesley's Covenant Service is adapted from *The Book of Worship* of The United Methodist Church.)[18]

Hymn #577 "God of Grace and God of Glory"

INVOCATION (Reader #1)

Almighty God, unto whom all hearts are open, all desires known, and from whom no secrets are hid: Cleanse the thoughts of our hearts by the inspiration of your Holy Spirit, that we may perfectly love you, and worthily magnify your holy name; through Jesus Christ our Lord. Amen.

INVITATION TO RENEWAL (Reader #2)

Sisters and brothers, the Christian life, to which we are called, is a life in Christ, realized in costly discipleship, and consecrated in the Spirit. Into this life we have been accepted fully, without reservation. This new covenant reflects the life of the Trinity: each person is related to the others, no one dominates, no one is subservient, but all are equal, free, responsible, and cooperating for the well-being of the entire community, enabling it to realize God's holy purpose.

(Reader #3)

This covenant is God's promise to fulfill in and through us the promise declared in Christ, the author and perfector of our faith. That this promise still stands we are sure, for we have known God's gracious goodness day by day.

(Reader #4)

In response, we pledge to live no more to ourselves, but to God who loves us and calls us to serve our disoriented, self-sufficient world, that we might be as Christ, empowered by the Spirit to become incarnations of God's holy promise.

(Reader #5)

Let us then, remembering the mercies of God and the hope of our calling, examine ourselves by the light of God's wisdom, that we may see where we have failed or fallen short in faith and practice, and considering all that this covenant means, give ourselves anew to God.

CONFESSION (Reader #1)

We are called to examine ourselves before God, humbly confessing our sin and watching our hearts, lest by self-deceit we shut ourselves out from God's presence. O God, we confess with shame our reluctance to follow Christ. Called by you, we do not heed. Faced with the beauty of all creation, we close our eyes. Challenged by hands that stretch out to us, we pass by.

HAVE MERCY UPON US AND FORGIVE US, O GOD.
(Read words in upper case in unison.)

(Reader #2)

You have blessed us with talents, spiritual gifts, our very being, yet, in false humility, we answer, "No, not I," or we try to do everything, sharing neither the work nor the blessings with others.

HAVE MERCY UPON US AND FORGIVE US, O GOD.

(Reader #3)

We have received love and faith from you, yet so little of your love reaches others through us. Forgive us for cherishing the things that divide us from others, being thoughtless in our judgments, hasty in condemnation, grudging in forgiveness.

HAVE MERCY UPON US AND FORGIVE US, O GOD.

(Reader #4)

Where we have failed—to tell the story, share the wealth, heal divisions, and cross boundaries of nation, language or ideas—

HAVE MERCY UPON US AND FORGIVE US, O GOD.
GIVER OF LIFE, BEARER OF PAIN, MAKER OF LOVE.
YOU ACCEPT WHAT WE CANNOT EVEN ACKNOWLEDGE IN
    OURSELVES;
YOU NAME WITHIN US WHAT WE CANNOT BEAR TO SPEAK;
YOU REMEMBER WHAT WE HAVE TRIED TO FORGET;
YOU REVEAL WHAT WE CANNOT EVEN CONCEIVE.
RECONCILE US THROUGH YOUR CROSS
TO ALL THAT WE HAVE REJECTED AND DEMEANED IN
    OURSELVES AND ONE ANOTHER,

THAT NO PART OF YOUR CREATION MAY SEEM ALIEN OR
STRANGE TO US,
AND THAT WE MAY BE MADE WHOLE IN YOU. AMEN.

PROCLAMATION OF THE WORD
First Reading: Genesis 12:1-3
Second Reading: Hebrews 12:1-2

RESPONSE TO THE WORD
Using excerpts from your journals, workbooks, and other notes,
share testimonies of images of the church, visions of service, and
commitments to grow in ministry.

Hymn #606 "Come, Let Us Use the Grace Divine"
(During the singing, have participants bring forward their covenants and/or prayer requests written earlier to present as an
offering, along with the presentation of the Communion elements.)

HOLY COMMUNION

(Reader #1)
O Gracious One, we give thanks for your loving kindness which
fills our days and brings us to this time and place.

WE PRAISE YOUR NAME, HOLY AND BLESSED TRINITY.

You have called us and blessed us, with life, reason, intuition, and
myriad other gifts. You have set us in a world which is full of your
glory. You have comforted us with kindred and friends, and
ministered to us through the minds and hands of our sisters and
brothers.

WE PRAISE THE MYSTERY OF YOUR WAYS, HOLY AND BLESSED
TRINITY.

(Reader #2)
You have set in our hearts a hunger for you, given us your peace,
redeemed us and called us to live deliberately—doing as Christ
did and being his Body. You have made us a community in your
Spirit and given us places of witness and service in the church
and in the world.

WE PRAISE YOUR LIFE, HOLY AND BLESSED TRINITY.

(Reader #3)

You have remembered us when we have forgotten you, followed us when we have fled from you, welcomed us when we returned to you. For your long-suffering and your grace,

WE PRAISE YOU, HOLY AND BLESSED TRINITY,
JOINING WITH YOUR PEOPLE OF ALL TIMES AND PLACES AND
  SAYING,
HOLY, HOLY, HOLY, GOD OF POWER AND MIGHT,
THE VAST EXPANSES OF SPACE RESOUND WITH YOUR GLORY.
BLESSED IS THE ONE WHO COMES IN THE NAME OF GOD.
LET ALL CREATION SING, HOSANNA!

(Reader #4)

We thank you for Jesus' life, and all he taught us of your love. We especially thank you for the meal he shared and asked us to celebrate until the end of time. When he was at supper with his friends, he took the bread, blessed you, called you Abba, and broke the bread, saying:

TAKE AND EAT. THIS IS MY BODY BROKEN FOR YOU.

Then he took the cup of wine, blessed you again, and passed it among the community saying:

TAKE AND DRINK, EVERYONE.
THIS IS THE CUP OF MY BLOOD POURED OUT FOR ALL.
DRINK THIS ALWAYS IN MEMORY OF ME.

And so we thank you, God our Creator, for in Christ's life we find the way from isolation to community, and from the illusion of self-sufficiency to the reality of interwoven love.

MAY THE HOLY SPIRIT RELEASE US FROM HIDING OUR GIFTS,
DENYING OUR SERVICE, AND REFUSING GOD'S GRACE.

SHARING THE BREAD AND CUP

The bread is passed from person to person, as they say to one another: "The Body of Christ, the food of baptized community."

The cup is passed, as each one says in turn: "The blood of Christ, the drink of overflowing blessing."

HYMN AFTER SHARING EUCHARIST
#614 "For the Bread Which You Have Broken"

INVITATION TO THE COVENANT (Reader #5)
And now, friends, let us bind ourselves with willing bonds to our covenant God, and take the yoke of Christ upon us.

We take Christ's yoke upon us

AND ARE HEARTILY CONTENT THAT GOD APPOINT US OUR PLACE AND WORK.

God has many services to be done; some are easy, others are difficult;

SOME BRING HONOR, OTHERS BRING REPROACH;

Some are suitable to our natural inclinations and temporal interests,

OTHERS ARE CONTRARY TO BOTH.

In some we may please God and please ourselves;

IN SOME WE CANNOT PLEASE GOD EXCEPT BY DENYING OURSELVES.

Yet the power to do all these things is assuredly given us. We have received the power of the Spirit, who strengthens us. Therefore let us make the covenant of God our own. Being thus prepared, let us now, in sincere dependence on God's grace and trusting in the promises of Jesus Christ, yield ourselves anew to God.

WE ARE NO LONGER OUR OWN, BUT YOURS.
PUT US TO WHAT YOU WILL, RANK US WITH WHOM YOU
    WILL;
PUT US TO DOING, PUT US TO SUFFERING;
LET US BE EMPLOYED FOR YOU OR LAID ASIDE FOR YOU,
EXALTED FOR YOU OR BROUGHT LOW FOR YOU;
LET US BE FULL, LET US BE EMPTY;
LET US HAVE ALL THINGS, LET US HAVE NOTHING;
WE FREELY AND HEARTILY YIELD ALL THINGS TO YOUR
PLEASURE AND DISPOSAL.

AND NOW, O GLORIOUS AND BLESSED GOD, HOLY TRINITY,
YOU ARE OURS, AND WE ARE YOURS, SO BE IT. AND THE
COVENANT WHICH WE HAVE MADE ON EARTH, LET IT BE
RATIFIED IN HEAVEN. AMEN.

Hymn #177 "He Is Lord"

APPENDIX
LEADER'S NOTES

This study incorporates elements of study, reflection, action, and worship within a design that allows for discovery and commitment by individuals and the group. As leader, you are a model participant each week. Allow yourself time each week to prepare all of the elements, undergirding your preparation with prayer, and opening yourself to the surprises and discoveries of God's Spirit in the midst of the people.

1. Read the text for each session ahead of time and prepare for discussion, activity, and worship.

2. All suggested hymns are from *The United Methodist Hymnal.* During preparation, decide what hymns to use. Have someone available and prepared who can accompany on piano or guitar or who can lead singing.

   NOTE: Other suggested hymns related to each of the major images of this study include the following: Body of Christ (550, 620, 552, 559, 560, 637); Servant (571, 582, 593, 712, 432, 344, 356, 434, 448); Growth in Grace (606, 375, 378, 416, 474, 512, 519).

3. Begin each session on time and with prayer. Encourage the participation of all members of the group. Arrange the space according to the format of the session, i.e., room for pairs or small groups to meet, space for doing artwork, etc.

4. Being part of a small group that has covenanted to continue through the study together should be a nurturing and edifying

experience. Meeting as a group allows an opportunity for relationships to grow. Time for informal interaction is helpful. Enjoy the discussion questions and other creative activities as a relaxing and lively time of fellowship together.

5. Collect covenant cards and prayer requests after the closing service. Plan to have group members use the prayer requests in individual devotional time or have the congregation lift up prayer requests during Sunday worship.

ENDNOTES

1. Richard Broholm, "The Call to Holy Worldliness: The Unfinished Reformation Agenda," *Centering,* Vol. I, No. 3 (Spring 1984), p. 6. Used by permission of the Center for the Ministry of the Laity, Newton Center, Mass.
2. *The COCU Consensus, In Quest of a Church of Christ Uniting,* 1985, pp. 43-44. Used with permission of Consultation on Church Union.
3. Thomas à Kempis, *The Imitation of Christ* (London: Penguin Books, 1973), p. 164. The adapted version appears in Morgan Noyes, *Prayers for Services* (New York: Scribner's, 1934), p. 150.
4. Charles V. Bryant, *Rediscovering the Charismata* (Waco, TX: Word, 1986), 66.
5. Keith S. Karlile, "Prayer," *alive now!* (September-October, 1989), p. 39. Used by permission.
6. Dottie Lovelady Rogers, "Litany of Responsibility," *alive now!* (January/February, 1980), p. 35. Used by permission of Dottie Lovelady Rogers, Wesley Foundation Director, Mobile, Alabama.
7. Stanley J. Menking, "Imago Dei: A Theology for the Ministry of the Laity" (unpublished manuscript, 1988), p. 4. Used by permission.
8. Archbishop Oscar Romero, *The Church Is All of You: Thoughts of Archbishop Oscar Romero.* Compiled and translated by James R. Brockman (Harper-Collins, 1984), 105.
9. Broholm, pp. 3, 4. Adapted with permission.
10. Letty M. Russell, *The Future of Partnership* (Philadelphia: Westminster Press, 1979), pp. 73-76.
11. Sudha Khristmukti, "I Care," *alive now!* (November-December 1988), Copyright © 1988 by The Upper Room. Used by permission.
12. *The United Methodist Hymnal* (The United Methodist Publishing House, 1989), #456.
13. *The Book of Discipline of The United Methodist Church, 1988* (Nashville: The United Methodist Publishing House, 1988), #201, p. 120. Used by permission.

14. John Wesley as quoted in R. W. Burtner and R. E. Chiles, eds., *A Compend of Wesley's Theology* (Nashville: Abingdon Press, 1954).
15. Henri Nouwen, *Gracias! A Latin American Journal* (San Francisco: Harper and Row, 1983), p. 187.
16. *The United Methodist Hymnal*, #481.
17. John Wesley, "A Covenant Prayer in the Wesleyan Tradition," *The United Methodist Hymnal*, #607.
18. _____, "Covenant Service" adapted by F. Willard Moffat for the United Methodist congregation at Old West Church in Boston, Massachusetts. See also: Hoyt Hickman et al., *Handbook of the Christian Year* (Nashville: Abingdon Press, 1986), p. 78.

FOR FURTHER READING

Adams, J. L. *The Prophethood of All Believers.* Beacon Press, 1985.

Broholm, Richard. "The Call to Holy Worldliness," *Centering,* Vol. I, No. 3 (Spring 1984).

_____ and Hoffman, John. *Empowering Laity for Their Full Ministry.* The Center for the Ministry of the Laity: Andover Newton Theological School, 1985.

Brown, Raymond. *The Church the Apostles Left Behind.* New York: Paulist Press, 1984.

Bryant, Charles V. *Rediscovering the Charismata.* Waco, Texas: Word Books, 1986.

Carter, William J. *Each One a Minister.* Nashville, TN: Discipleship Resources, 1986.

Dozier, Verna. *Equipping the Saints.* The Alban Institute, 1987.

_____. *The Authority of the Laity.* The Alban Institute, 1982.

Dulles, Avery. *Models of the Church.* New York: Doubleday, 1987.

Edge, Findley. *The Greening of the Church.* Waco, Texas: Word Books, 1971.

Gibbs, Mark and T. Ralph Morton. *God's Lively People.* Philadelphia: Westminster Press, 1971.

Hanson, Paul. *The People Called.* San Francisco: Harper & Row, 1986.

Hawkins, Thomas R. *Building God's People.* Nashville, TN: Discipleship Resources, 1990.

Kinghorn, Kenneth Cain. *Gifts of the Spirit.* Nashville: Abingdon, 1976.

Mather, Herb. *Gifts Discovery Workshop.* Nashville: Discipleship Resources, 1985.

Mead, Loren B. *Lay Ministry, a Tool Kit.* The Alban Institute, 1983.

Minear, Paul. *Images of the Church in the New Testament.*

Morris, Margie. *Seven Reasons to Volunteer.* Nashville, TN: Discipleship Resources, 1989.

Nouwen, Henri. *¡Gracias!, a Latin American Journal.* San Francisco: Harper & Row, 1983.

Outler, Albert, ed. *John Wesley.* New York: Oxford University Press, 1964.

Peck, George and Hoffman, John. *The Laity in Ministry.* Valley Forge, PA: Judson Press, 1984.

Purdy, John. *Returning God's Call.* Louisville, KY: Westminster/John Knox Press, 1989.

Rhodes, Lynn. *Co-creating: A Feminist Vision of Ministry.* Philadelphia: Westminster Press, 1987.

Romero, Oscar. *The Church Is All of You: Thoughts of Archbishop Oscar Romero.* Compiled and translated by James Brockman. Minneapolis: Winston Press, 1984.

Russell, Letty M. *The Future of Partnership.* Philadelphia: Westminster Press, 1979.

Vos, Nelvin. *Monday Ministries.* Philadelphia: Parish Life Press, 1979.

Watson, David Lowes. *Covenant Discipleship.* Nashville: Discipleship Resources, 1991.